T0128352

FOCUS ON REASON

A DEIST SPEAKS HIS MIND

FOR THOSE NOT AFRAID TO THINK

RICHARD NORMAN

ISBN: 978-1-4669-0105-6 (sc)
ISBN: 978-1-4669-0106-3 (e)

Trafford rev. 03/28/2012

 www.trafford.com

North America & International
toll-free: 1 888 232 4444 (USA & Canada)
phone: 250 383 6864 ♦ fax: 812 355 4082

To Shawn, Tyawn and Fred

Thanks

LET US BE TRANSFORMED
BY THE RENEWAL OF OUR MINDS

Romans 12: 2

_____

_____

The footnotes found on this subject are
Conflicting therefore non were used

PART 1

"The Rest of Us"

INTRODUCTION

An open letter to the biblical God;

I'm not taking responsibility for any of this. You did it, you clean it up. Don't try to cloud the issue with a lot of rhetoric; you did it, you clean it up. I'm going to be the best person I can be and you take it from there. Don't tell me you tried to clean it up by sending your Son down here because your creation killed him too.

Jesus didn't die for me, I didn't do anything; I wasn't even here then. You said, "Jesus died so that I may have eternal life," Well, I don't want eternal life, Life isn't that great. The few laughs you get out of life, doesn't compensate for the aggravation.

Furthermore, I never understood exactly what it is we are supposed to do in Heaven, other than sit.

FOREWORDS

If we are comfortable in our beliefs, who are you to sow seeds of doubt? Why muddy the water when the pool is calm? What gives you that right? I have no right. What I have is a strong conviction that makes me feel compelled to share these insights with you and if by sharing these insights with you, it helps you to realize a higher truth, a greater truth, and a stronger conviction of the existence of God—and this realization helps you to be more persuasive when exchanging ideas with the unformed or the misinformed, then I feel THE REST OF US would benefit from the experience—for these insights are based on God's realities and not on any particular religious persuasion.

In as much as being a Christian is a wonderful thing, I want you to fully understand what I mean when I use the term Christian. I mean as Christ like as possible, I mean accepting Jesus Christ as your personal savior, I mean believing in the virgin birth, the resurrection, and the crucifixion and letting Jesus Christ into your life whereby the Holy Spirit dictate your conduct. I mean walking with Jesus stride for stride, as you march up the Kings Highway. When the going gets tough and you have done all you can and you still can not see your way, believing you only have to call on Jesus and say, "Jesus; I have done all I can, It's in your hands now," Can't you see what a comfort this is—to go through life knowing you have Jesus on your side, knowing, regardless of what happens, you are not along.

When I say Christian, I do not mean being religious or being a churchgoer, for there is a difference. A religious person is one who can quote the Bible, chapter and verse and not have a clue as to its meaning. They have heard these verses so often they have them committed to memory.

A "churchgoer" is one who goes to church religiously every Sunday Morning, They usually go to churches with large congregations where they can see and be seen. But what about **THE REST OF US?,** What about those of us who go to church but give little thought to what we hear? Who go to church because we believe God is going to bless us with material things? With two thirds of the children of the world going to bed hungry every night, I'm sure God has more important things to do than seeing to it that you get the television, car or home of your dreams. There are others who would like to believe in God but their intelligence gets in the way. When you ask a true Christian, "How do you know you are going to heaven when you die?" Their response is because the Bible tells me so and I believe in the Bible." I'm sure all of us would like to be in the kind of comfort zone that Christianity provides but have a problem believing in the Bible. Many of us join Bible Study groups in order to learn more about the Christian Doctrine. Before we can select a Study Group, we must first decide which Bible we should study. The Gutenberg Bible of 1456 or the Tyndale Bible of 1535

The Cranner Bible of 1541, The Geneve Bible of 1572, The King James verison of 1603, Then comes the Amplified Bible of 1954, Not to mention the Catholic Bible, The Mormon's Bible, now known as the (The Church Of Jesus Christ Of latter Day Saints), The Jehovah Witness Bible or the Apocrypha, which are the books the (constituted authority) decided should not appear in what is now considered the Holy Bible. Regardless of the selection, they all claim to be the words of God. All these Bibles are different interpretations of the same teachings of Christ.

I have yet to mention the other religions such as Hinduism, Buddhism, Confucianism, Taoism (Dow), Islam, Judaism, etc.

At the Nazarene Bible College in Point Loma California, we studied the Exegesis of the Hermeneut's—(in plan English), it means, the interpretation of the translation of the Old Testament from Hebrew to Greek. So you see how easy it would be to come away more confused, than when you began. If you are going to study the Bible, please know what you are about and for God sakes, know something about the person who is teaching you. You don't want to end up with a Pastor like Jim Jones, drinking cool aid laced with cyanide or a David Koreasch, of the Waco Texas fires or with Do and Ra of Heavens Gate, on a cot with a scarf over your face, waiting to catch the tail end of the next comet.

The Bible is a very sophisticated literary work and like all literary works you have to understand its purpose and what it is trying to convey. Many of us would not even consider reading the writings of Shakespeare, Shaw or Longfellow because we say it is too difficult to understand, yet we will read the Bible and swear we understand every word. You do not have to study the Bible to be a Christian. God existed long before the Bible was written. Doing right is self evident; no one has to tell you when you are doing wrong. Many Pastors would have you study the Bible year after year, as though you were going to get a degree.

One day as I was conversing with my eighty seven year old Mother In law, I asked, "Where are you going," she said, "to Sunday School." I asked, "What are you taught in Sunday" School?" she said, "I am taught about The Bible," How long have you been going to Sunday School?" She said, "Since I was six years old," I said, "If you have been studying the Bible for eighty-one years, I am sure by now, you have learned all these lessons can teach and you should give your seat to someone less knowledgeable. Yet she still goes to Church and pores over those same scriptures Sunday after Sunday.

Many of us are not literate enough to fully understand the parables, allegories and metaphors, found in the Bible, nor, do we need to be. It is not necessary to be an intellectual giant to understand Christ's Ministry. He tells us to avoid foolish questions, generalities and contentions, for they are unprofitable and vain."(Titus 3:9).

"Let not your heart be troubled, ye believe in God, believe also in Me,"(John 14:1), "Come unto to me all ye that labor and are heavy laden and I will give you rest", "Take my yoke upon you, and learn of me; for I am meek and lowly in heart and ye shell find rest unto your souls, for my yoke is easy and my burden is light."

Matt 11; 28-30.

When the lawyers asked Jesus, "what is the greatest commandment," Jesus said, "thou shall love the Lord thy God with all thy heart, soul, mind and body, this is the greatest commandment and the second is liken unto the first, thou shall love thy neighbor as thyself, On these two commandments hang all the laws of the prophets," (Matt 22: 36 through 40). Jesus is saying, "It is not worship or praise, it is conduct."

It is how you conduct yourself toward your fellow Man. All the laws are fulfilled in these words. Thou shall love thy neighbor as thy self," (Gal, 5:14). "My reward is with me to give every man according to their works." Rev 22: 12.

When you love God and keep His commandments, you will be blessed, not with cars, a new home, job, husband or wife, for these things can be taken away from you. When God blesses you, his blessings can not be taken away from you, For God blesses you with Peace, Joy, Long suffering (Patience) and a quiet mind. "Let us hear the conclusion of this matter, Fear God and keep His Commandments, for this is the whole duty of man—to love ye one another as I have loved you." Eccles. 12:1. Be still and know that I am God. Psalm 46:10.

Although the fellowship, praise and worshiping, done on Sunday Morning by people of the same persuasion is up lifting, Jesus said the greatest praise you can give God is through your conduct toward your fellow man. All else is superfluous.

In order to keep down confusion, I would like to explain to you what I mean when I use the word God. The term is a synonym for First Cause, Divine Intelligence, Supreme Being and That, That Is Responsible, For All.

CONCEPT

Because nature (natural law) functions without any assistance from mankind, many feel that nature is first cause (God) however; I feel that God is responsible for all including nature. Therefore, If God is omnipotent (all powerful), omniscient (all knowing) and omnipresent (ever present) and is responsible for all, then man is innocent, if man is guilty, than God is not all powerful. I can not accept the God described in the Bible for the same reasons I can not accept Leprechauns, Mother Goose or the Tooth Fairy. Were I to acknowledge the Biblical reference to Angels and demons as being part of reality, then I must also accept Tinkerbelle and Peter Pan as having a real or actual existence.

Our religious concepts are among the worst ever conceived by the minds of man and are obviously mistaken. By religion, I don't mean Catholic, Protestant, Baptist, etc. as they are only different interpretation of the same religion. I mean all religions; Buddhism, Taoism (Dow) Hinduism, Confucianism, Islam, Judaism, etc. are not only mistaken but they are harmful because these religions come between Human Beings and their concept of the Supreme.

Grant, Mankind needs spiritual fulfillment but this is a personal thing between Man, his God and how he perceives Him.

For an institution, religious or otherwise, to assume they have the right to come between Man and his God, to interpret God for Him is criminal and to claim they are authorize by God to do this, is a disservice. Then to pray on Man's instinctive superstitious nature, in order to maintain and sustain the very institution responsible for most of his ills is a disgrace. To justify this self appointed authority over the messes, all the religions invented a Christ of one sort or another, (Christianity being unique, for it is the only religion that claims their Christ to be God, Man and the Holy Spirit all wrapped up in one) and that this Christ died for our sins. The fact that Christianity claims Christ Died for us is supposed to justify this institution's involvement in all facets of our lives. They even go so far as to invade the privacy of our bedrooms and dictate how we are to conduct ourselves. This is not only depraved, it's rude. The explanation goes, we must do as our religions dictate in order to get along with God and if we get along we God, then we will automatically get along with one another. This is their answer to the Human dilemma. I contend the reverse is more likely true, if we get along with each other, this should satisfy even the Gods Conceived by our religions.

We must grant that any deity, energy, power, God or what ever you want to call it, capable of producing anything as mathematically precise as this universe, is worth of all the praise and obedience we can give. The hang up is, just how does one go about it?

RESPECT

Respect is not difficult to give the Supreme, for it is a natural reaction. As long as our actions are directed toward sustaining life, we are respecting the giver of life. In order to disrespect the giver of life, one would have to be a destroyer of life—which is unnatural because one who destroys life makes the possibility of their own destruction more real. Suicide is the ultimate disrespect, for you are destroying something not of your making.

So you see respect is within our ability to understand. Praise and obedience is a little more difficult to deal with. In order to praise this Supreme Intelligence, certain unknown must be assumed. We must assume we know this Supreme Intelligence well enough to know what it would like to hear. The first prerequisite to successful praising is it must be pleasing to the ear. That the Supreme has an ear at all is pure conjecture.

Would it not be more honest to admit that with the exception of its existence, we know nothing at all about this Supreme Intelligence?—Therefore does it no logically follow that it would be impossible to praise it? How arrogant of us to assume the Supreme Intelligence is as we are, vain, jealous, envious, revengeful and responding to these emotions as we do. This is second only to suicide in disrespect.

Religious Beings in their astronomical conceit, equate all things according to their understanding. What is beyond their understanding must be reduced to their leave of comprehension or discarded as nonexistent. If the Supreme Intelligence (which is obviously far beyond our own) can not—for superstitious reasons, be discarded, then we must reduce this Intelligence to within our ability to understand. For to admit something exist beyond our understanding, is to take the agnostic position that no one knows, thus we could no longer call our selves Christians. Does it not logically follow that it would be impossible to praise it? Why must we in our attempt to glorify God, always disparage Him? When we are not disparaging God in an attempt to make Him understandable, we are belittling His creation; Man. They say that Man is of a sinful nature, therefore imperfect. What we are saying is "from perfection came imperfection". Will we ever learn that it is not necessary to belittle Mankind in order to glorify God? In face the reverse is more likely, the greater the creation the greater the creator. The only way to praise God is through conduct.

OBEDIENCE

Obedience denotes submission—compliance with a command
to abstain from what is forbidden or to yield willingly to what is
asked of us. These definitions are not incorrect, only incomplete, for
you can not have obedience without authority. The logical question
here is to what and for what? The religious answer is to God, for
allowing us to experience the gift of life. It is impossible to show our
appreciation through obedience, for we know not the command.
We are told these commands are revealed in the beautiful prose
and poetic sonnets found in the Holy Bible—produce by so called
divinely inspired men. A Supreme Intelligence capable of creating
the universe and everything therein could not have inspired these
scriptures regardless of their beauty, for they do not deal with the
whole Human Being and his universe. They lack peripheral vision,
this is understandable when you consider the fact that the disciples
and scribes responsible for these scriptures were narrow minded men,
necessarily so, for these men never traveled more than a hundred
miles from there place of birth. Paul was the exception. Although
he was educated and well traveled, his epistles only explained his
understanding of the writings of others. They wrote as thou they

were viewing the world through a key hole, all periphery was eliminated. Their concepts are far to narrow to encompass the whole of Mankind and his confrontation with his universe. Therefore it follows, that they could not possibly be inspired by a God that is responsible for all. Anything we can do to sustain the existence of life on this planet is obviously in accord with God's plan, for we only exist through His will. If God did not want us to exist, He would only have to will it so. Our obsession is our inability to understand the why (or the essence) of our existence. Why do we exist if the only certainty is that we will cease too? Why bother to establish life on this planet at all, when the laws of nature are allowed to destroy all life with the passing of time? If logic and reason were applied to these known, it would follow that living is a dying process. If reason concludes this to be true, then why bother with life at all? There is only one intelligent answer, **we do not know because it is beyond our understanding.** Can't you see how this attitude frees us to grapple with our dilemma—realizing that the elimination of evil is outside the realm of Human possibility—but not letting that fact deter us from striving to make the fact of evil less so. We should take what we can and make of this world what we will—free of all guilt, superstitions, religions, etc. facing the end result proudly, whatever it might be, acknowledging the result to be the best that we can do considering what we had to work with, which is ourselves.

Belief in a deity that is involved in our every-day lives on this planet is unreasonable, for there is no evidence of this. Our logic and reason tell us that if this manipulative deity exists at all, it is dormant, so why the obedience? Why the obligation? The statement, "not my but thy will be done" is unnecessary because it infers it is possible to do other than God's will. If this is true, God could not possibly be all powerful, for powers would exist outside of His. Satan only has the power God gave him (if *he* exists at all). Many of us feel that by not doing what God will's us to do (as if this were possible), we render ourselves unworthy but what it is we are unworthy of, escapes me. Is it the promise of salvation? Is it our awareness—(the ability to discern for our selves what is good)? I recognize no obligation for these abilities. They were not requested, my conscience found itself in possession of faculties not of my choosing, so why the reverence? Why must I be made to feel the need to atone for something I don't understand?

GOD, A HUMAN CREATION

Through speculation, rationalization and expectation, we have created a religion and a God to reside over it. Being ignorant and limited in our knowledge of such things, Mankind conceived of a God in Man's own image.—With all the Human short comings. We created a God that is jealous, conceited, vindictive, cruel and selfish—possessing all of the emotions we find in ourselves. This is understandable because to conceive of an entity unlike ourselves is inconceivable. Since we cannot know the truth of God, (we only believe) why not create a God we can know, one who appeals to our concept of logic and reason—one who is within our ability to understand?

It is the God born of Man's religious superstitions who tells us that happiness comes through choice. The theory dictates that Man is given the choice of good or evil and the fact that he chooses good, rather than evil, of his own free will, is suppose to put us in sync with God. For the life of me, I cannot understand all this so called choice. When did we ever have a choice? Were we taken aside and given a short synopsis of what our lives would be like, the choice of parents, place of birth, appearance, ancestry, abilities—the choice of being born or remaining in our Mother's womb, enjoying the comfort of a sensual utopia—the choice to be or not to be? The answer is an emphatic no. The only choice the God Man created, claim to have given us, pertain to good or evil. However, there is little personal choice involved here as well. Natural law is responsible for the genealogy that influenced our appearance. Whether we are to be tall, shore, fat or lean, is settled as conception and before birth, along with intelligence and aptness. Our personalities are influenced by the social environment we find our selves exposed to. Before the age of seven, our personalities are fully developed. The kind of person we will be, concepts, desires, etc., are acquired though education (or the lack there of), as we go through life. Education can only broaden the perspectives of a personality that was fully developed before the educational process began. So you see, we are product of our environment more than any thing else. We are no more responsible for our preference, desires or choices than we are for the color for our hair, eyes, or skin.

Within any culture, we are only exposed to certain concepts. Only those very unique individuals, with an extremely sophisticated education and a will of iron, can brake through the façade of so-called education as taught in our Western Culture, to the ecstasy of free thought, which must be the forerunner of free choice. At a famous meeting of the Free Religious Association of America, held in Boston during the letter part of the nineteenth century, a some what over zealous minister quoted certain passages from the gospels, adding that these scriptures could not be matched in the sacred books of any other religions. At this point, Ralph Waldo Emerson, who was in the audience, rose and quietly said, "The gentleman's remarks only prove how narrowly he has read."

Some years ago, Stanley Kramer produce a movie called, "The Defiant Ones, featuring Tony Curtis and Sidney Portiea. This movie made our interdependence quite clear. Two convicts, one white, one black, who were mortal enemies, made so by their exposure to our racist culture, escaped from prison but were unable to free themselves from the chains that bound them together. Throughout the movie, the point was made that, although these men hated each other, they had to work together in order to remain free. By working together, they soon realized their survival depended on them realizing the need they had for one another. We can all learn from the Defiant On

SURVIAL

The attempt to survive and procreate is as nature as breathing and also Godly. Our religions take issue with this. They claim that Mankind has another purpose in life other than survival and that is to worship. They have sat down certain rituals we must follow, such as going to church and praying for salvation from the sin of being born and if we conduct ourselves in such a way as to be saved, we will be taken out of this world to a heaven where the Christ presides. When salvation is mentioned, any one in their right mind would think of being saved from the onslaught of nature. Were it not for our doctors and scientists, nature would have a free hand at killing us a little each day.

We are supposed to happily forego the God given gift of life on this earth in anticipation of being with Christ in Heaven. Our love for Him is supposed to be greater than our love of life, for it is said; He died on the cross for our sins. Many men have been known to lay down their lives for their fellow man. Spartacus gave his life fighting for man who were enslaved and for the idea of freedom. All who followed him and were caught alive were crucified but there lives were not mercifully snuffed out by a spear in the side to spare then the agony of hanging on the cross until dead. Socrates gave his life for the noblest cause of all, Truth! To give one's life in the defense of truth is the highest good. Joan Of Arc, at the age of nineteen, was convicted and burned at the stake because she believed she was responsible to God and not the Church of Rome for her conduct, Doctor Martin Luther King Junior, through his nonviolent approach, was able to get America, (the most powerful country in the world) to change it's raciest policies without one single act of violence. He said, "If blood must flow because of this quest, let it be mine." Dr. Martin Luther King helped America come closer to its image as the land of the free. I could name more, but I think this makes my point.

These people gave their lives for what they believed in without any idea of regaining that life after death. I cannot feel eternally grateful to Jesus without being grateful to all the others who gave their lives for their fellow Man and for what they believed in. To claim Jesus feat was unique because it save us from Hell's fire is conjecture, for we have no evidence that hell's fire exist. Alice K. Turner, author of The History of Hell, attributes the origin of the concept of Hell, to Mesopotamia, some four thousand years ago. However, it was Zoroaster, a Persian religious teacher in the sixth century before Christ, who developed a more sophisticated approach to the belief that there would be a day of reckoning whereby our good and bad deeds would be considered before it is determined whether we are to go to heaven or to hell's fires after death. According to the Torah, those who do not qualify for immediate acceptance into Gan Eden (the garden of Eden—also know as Heaven) must begin the process of cleansing called Sheol, "one of the seven chambers of Gehinom, aka. Hell" This process is painful but is necessary to restore the soul to the purity it experienced before entering the physical world. Only after this method of purification is complete, can the soul be allowed to enter Gan Eden, (The Garden Of Eden) Heaven. However, none of this can be found in the Bible used by the Christian religion.

About two thousand one hundred years ago, A Jew from Galilee called Jesus The Christ, made the coming of a new world, consisting of a Heaven and a Hell, the focal point of his ministry, (however Judaism does not subscribe to this concept of Hell nor do they recognize Jesus as the Messiah promised by the Prophets in the Old Testament.)

LOGIC

There can be no logical explanation for the Christian doctrine because it is a belief and if that belief becomes knowledge, then there would be no need for faith, which is the basis of the whole thing. Christianity is not a reasonable conclusion one can logically defend in an intellectual debate. Any one who attempt to do so, does Christianity a disservice. Theologians unwittingly aid the antagonists when they try to do so. This approach only cause confusion because Christianity is not logical or reasonable, nor is it supposed to be. As I said before, it is a belief base on faith. To approach this subject logically, to grope for a reasonable explanation, to try to know the unknowable, is to weaken the basic structure the religion is founded on. To acquire knowledge or to know, eliminate any need for belief. Therefore, it follows that knowledge eliminate any need for faith because their can not be any belief. God (or what ever it was that created us), gave us the ability to recall past experiences and through these recollections we are aware of what we experienced. It is to know through experience that enable us to record for posterity the knowledge accumulated over time and pass this information on to future generations—unlike any other species on earth.

If I had just return from the post office and was asked its whereabouts, I would know because I would have experience being there. Now that I know where it is, I can pass this information on. Anyone asking me the whereabouts of the post office, must rely on their belief that I know what I'm talking about when I tall them and have faith enough in that belief to follow my instructions. They will know my directions were correct only after they get there. Until then, they can only act on their faith in their belief that I am telling them the truth. If they knew the way, there would be no need for faith in my directions. Belief is not knowledge. Many of us have trouble distinguishing between the two. When we feel we know, we have no need for belief. Belief only applies to thing not experienced—things outside the realm of comprehension, (I don't know, so I will believe or disbelieve until I have satisfied myself that, yes this is truth and is known by me or no it is not true and is discarded), So you see to know or to think you know, makes belief impossible. For any one to imply he has a logical explanation for Christianity is dishonest. To apply logic and reason to Christianity is intellectual suicide. There is no logic whatsoever in the concept of the Holy Trinity and those among us who claim to understand this concept intellectually is lacking in honesty. Either accept Christianity for what it is, (*FAITH IN A PARTICULAR BELIEF*), or leave it alone.

THEOLOGY

The Israelites history, traditions and laws are called the Torah and the Talmud and can be found in parts of the Old Testament. The disciplines described in those thirty nine books are the basis of Judaism. This religion originated with Abraham (Called Abram at that time). Abraham was born in the city called Ur, in the southern part of Mesopotamia, now known as Iraq. Abraham was the first Monotheist. He was the first man to accept the oneness of God. Prior to Abraham's revelation, Polytheism was the religion of the day in that part of the world. Polytheism is the worship of several different Gods and Idols.

It was not until the emperor of Roman, Constantine The Great, accepted Jesus the Christ and imposed the Nicene Creed, (the relief in the Holy Trinity) was Christianity established as the official religion of Roman. The other Kings and Queens of Europe accepted the new religion by, 1096 A.D. The Pope of the Catholic Church persuades the King and Queens of Europe that it was their Christian duty to amass an army and take back the Holy Land from the so-called Islamic Infidels. Between the years 1096 and 1270

A.D, the Royalty of Europe sponsored ten crusades. These armies were called crusaders. The first crusade launched by Pope Urban the second succeeded in recapturing Jerusalem in 1099. Muslim armies recaptured Jerusalem in 1144 A.D. creating the need for a second crusade—that was unsuccessful. The third crusade, lunched in 1189 involved Richard the Lion Hearted of England who did not capture Jerusalem but manage to negotiate a peace treaty with Saladin, the head of the Muslim army that recaptured Jerusalem in 1187 A.D. The fourth crusade was a mess; it ended up with Catholic and Orthodox Christians fighting each other. This separation remains to this day. The fifth crusade, although a military victory was turned into a defeat because of the arrogance of Cardinal Pelagius, who gave the captured land back to the Muslins. The sixth crusade leads by Roman Emperor Fredrick the Second, in 1228 A.D., finely succeeded in Christians gaining authority over Jerusalem. The eight, ninth and tenth, crusades were disasters. The purpose of these crusades is not clear.

From two hundred A.D. to Nine hundred A.D., the Middle East was occupied primarily by Christians. Mohammad, in his quest to spread this new religion called Islam, invaded these lands and conquered most of them. The crusades were the Christians response to these invasions.

RELIGION

Human Beings could easily be made to realize the need we have for one another but for one insurmountable obstacle, religion. Religion since its inception has produced tragic consequences. This never ending battle that is raging in the Middle East today, that has claim so many innocent lives along with the lives of several coalition solders, who are predominantly American, will never end until we realize that this has been going on, ever since Abraham sent Hagar away with her baby Ishmael. According to Biblical History, God promised to make a great nation from the descendants of Ishmael. He also promised to make a great nation from the descendants of Isaac as well. From that day on, the Arabs and the Jews/Christians have been at each others throats constantly. If the crusades taught us anything, it is that we can not resolve these conflicts by force.

The use or misuse of religion has sired atrocities that defy the imagination. To think that there is a religion that can persuade Men to forego the gift of lift and embrace the promised of seventy two virgins in the after life, is an insult to Man ability to think—and to whole so strongly to these beliefs that they have no remorse when hundreds of innocent people are killed in their quest for these virgins.

The wanton destruction of the American Indian's culture, the rape and pillage of their land and the slaughter of their food supply, along with the inhuman treatment of the Men and Women of Africa when brought here as slaves, are examples of what Man has done in the name of Christian Evangelism. The Christian Religion, justify this conduct by saying, "we were merely bringing the Heathens to Christ". This could lead one to conclude that religion does more harm than good and should be indicted on the grounds that it has little real value and serves no useful purpose.

Our religious doctrines are not the answer, they are little more than psychedelic escapes from the reality of the ever now, riding on the wings of ideological nonsense, to the redemptive shores of things hoped for. It is for the many an opium, a necessary escape, a distortion of the real—like sunglasses, though far more harmful. The attempt by communism to systematize evil out of existence by satisfying only the physical side of Mankind was one of the reasons it failed. Granted the physical side of Man needs fulfilling, but the spiritual side of Man needs fulfillment as well. Let us fill that need with something of value, something that satisfies. Modern scholars, by and large, now are agreed that the Gospel of Jesus Christ offered an exemplified way of life which, if believed and adopted, would result in a Kingdom of heaven on earth where justice and love would reign. However, not until we realize the need we have for one another, will this higher life with God here on earth occur.

It is not my intention to debunk Christianity or any other religion, for there is more than enough literature doing just that. My purpose is to get us to realize the tragedy we are making of the gift of life and the injustice we are doing to God or (whatever it is that created us). The cliché, "life can be beautiful," is outside the realm of Human possibility only because we allow it to be so. Most of us live lives of quiet desperation because we accept all the old prejudices, taboos and superstitions as necessary ingredients for the good life. In this way, we have reduced life to a burdensome, guilt-ridden, self-reproaching existence of constant atonement—not worthy of the effort it takes to sustain it. We must wake up and use that portion of our brain that is submerged beneath layer of religious dogma brought on be religious indoctrination which is the opposite of education. Only then will we be able to recognize a theology compatible with our ability to understand—one that we can adhere to without hypocrisy. THE REST OF US, are still in a flux, trying to experience God through faith and belief rather than logic and reason. These contrasts are an oxymoron—they don't mix.

Until we realize the insignificance if salvation, we can never appreciate the magnificence of life. So long as we remain awed by the beauty and splendor of life and fascinated by the Human experience, the essence (or reason) for our existence is unimportant. We must relegate salvation to its rightful place behind the Human experience and accept the fact of its unimportance.

VALIDITY

Before we accept the Bible as the answer to the Human Dilemma, it would behoove us to examine it more closely. A God capable of creating anything as magnificent as this universe and everything their in, should be able to sponsor a book that is more convincing. Granted, the Holy Bible continues to sell well over fifty five million copies each year. This is fifty million more than the all time best seller," Gone With The Wind," and "How To Win Friends And Influence People." It can be argued that much of its appeal is due to the eroticism found in the many stories dealing with rape, incest, sadism, masturbation, adultery and prostitution. These actions merely are referred to as they relate to the various stories but are seldom described as deplorable. That the sexually erotic conduct found in the scriptures was somehow able to survive the most puritanical narrow-minded periods of antiquity is surprising to all but the few who profess to understand such things.

When evaluating the validity of the Bible, we must first take into consideration the allegories, parable, synonyms and metaphors, found in the Septuagint, (the oldest translation of the Bible from Hebrew to Greek), had been exposed to the economic and political systems of that day. That fact along with the different translation and interpretations, makes these translations suspect.

The writing of the Bible took forty authors fifteen hundred years, to record the more than four thousand years of history that described the culture, history and laws of the Jewish People. These scribes also included in their works, the Pentateuch, (the first five books of the Old Testament), the Gospel and the acts of a unique group of people called Christians. This belief spread from the Middle East, to Southern Europe and parts of Western Asia. As Paul and his follower neglected to include Africa, and the Near East in their travels, these areas succumbed to the teaching of Islam, brought to them by Mohammed who many believe to be a messenger from Allah (God). His followers are called Muslim. Paul's reasons for not including these areas are not clear.

Saul was a Roman Jew from the city of Tarsus, which is in the south eastern part of Turkey. While in route to Damascus, Saul experienced a revelation he believed came from Jesus The Christ. Saul believed this vision was a mandate from Christ to spread the Gospel throughout the world. However, scholars agree that throughout this vision, Jesus asked nothing of Saul—Jesus merely posed the question, "Saul, Saul, why persecute thou me?" It was Ananias, another disciple, who had a vision and was told, he should reveal to Saul, (now called Paul), that he would be the messenger responsible for spreading the Gospel to the rest of the world. Paul accepted a message brought to him by another.

However, it was Peter, one of the disciples who walked and talked with Jesus, who was given the command to establish the Christian

Church within the Jewish community and continue his ministry by saying, "Upon This Rock I Build My Church," Paul received no such command. As Paul had no apostolic authority and was not directly instructed By Christ to do anything, he was free to interpret what he perceived to be a divine revelation, any way he saw fit. I find it interesting that Paul decided to bring this new Religion to Southern Europe and parts of Western Asia while ignoring the rest of the world. That Paul chose to visit these areas four times while disregarding the rest of the world, leads one to believe his intention were to spread this new religion to those countries where he was comfortable with the culture and more familiar with the language. Were Paul divinely inspired by God, I am sure God would have suggested he visit other areas of the world as well.

The Bible consisted of sixty six books. The first thirty nine books are called the "Old Testament." They are the History, Prophesies and laws of the Hebrew People who practice the Jewish faith. The remaining twenty seven books are called, "The New Testament," The first four chapters are know as the Gospel, it consist of the telling and retelling of the doing of the man called Jesus, who was thought to be the messiah promised in the Old Testament. Jesus teachings were recorded by Matthew, Mark, Luke, and John. Only Matthew and John were companions of Jesus. Luke never saw him at all. It is believed that Mark may have seen him but he was not one of the twelve disciples. Only two of the writers of the Gospel were eye witnesses. The others two acquired their information years later through hearsay. God only knows where Paul got his information from. Whether it can to him through delusional insight or divine revelation, Paul felt he was the man chosen to explain everything. Jesus came to fulfill the prophecies promised in the Old Testament. He did not come to create a new religion. It was Paul who took it upon himself to form a new religion (although the name came later). Paul replaced the basic tenet of Christ's teachings (which was very simple), "Believe In God And Love Thy Neighbor as thy self." Paul said "good works are not enough. For they in and of themselves, are as filthy rags."

CHRONOLOGY

The chronology according to the Judeo Christian historians is as follows; Adam, 4000 + B.C.E., Noah unknown?, Abraham, 2000 B,C,E, Moses, 1500 B.C.E. David, 1000 B.C.E. and then came Jesus, 0000. The Gospel and the Epistles of Paul were written within the first hundred years after the death of Christ and after the life and times of Ezra, Nehemiah and Esther. About 250 B.C.E., a collection of fourteen, (some say more), ancient Jewish writings called the Apocrypha, appeared, Although these books are accepted by the Roman Catholic Church as divinely inspired, they do not appear in the Holy Bible. This clearly confirms that what arrears in the Bible, is the result of decisions made by religious leaders who felt they had the ecclesiastical knowledge and the canonized authority to determine what books should or should not appear in the Bible. They legitimized their decisions by arguing that the scriptures they allowed to appear did not contradict academically approved recorded history. The fact that Mankind's so—called divinely inspired scriptures do not contradict Mankind's history does not validate the claim they are the words of God, it only confirms mankind's preconceived conclusions.

ATHEISTS

By no means do I feel qualified to speak for anyone other than my self but it is my understanding that most Atheists are vehemently opposed to the Biblical concept of God. Nonbelievers, (The Rest of Us), do not reject the existence of something greater than Man, (for to do so is to insult one's own intelligence), God, is present by the various religions. We resent the so-called divinely inspired religious leaders who present God as a product that is manufactured, advertised, package and sold to anyone seeking spiritual understanding. These religious leaders write their own agenda, operate outside the realm of anti-trust laws, pay no taxes and enjoy total autonomy in all they do. It is a profit oriented industry without any restrictions whatsoever. As these privileges are only extended to religious entities; they have become the richest organizations in the Western World.

For Atheism to deny the existence of God is to question one's own existence, for it is obvious we did not create our selves. Most non-believers say, "I would like to believe but my intelligence gets in the way." This posed the question, is their any concept of God that would not insult our intelligence, one that is void of hypocrisy and contradictions? The answer is yes.

First we must grant that God's truths are universal and not subject to change. What Mankind observes as Change in the universe is not change but responses to the cycles of natural-law put in place by a Supreme Intelligence that dictates; That for every action, their must an equal and opposite reaction. In order for something to live, something must die. With God's natural law, all things are constant. With Human Beings the only constant is change. Therefore, does it not logically follow that sin is a Human assumption? Its inconsistencies leave no doubt as to it origin.

Christian Bible dictionaries, defines sin as "a willful violation of religious or moral principles," this concept of sin is in a constant state of flux, brought on by the social/economic conditions one finds in any given period of recorded history. Sin is whatever a particular culture says; it is—based on what those cultures decided right moral conduct or religious principles are at that point in time.

Our gathering of information is ongoing and as we become more aware of our ignorance, we realize that truth for Humanity not is absolute. What is true for Mankind today may not be true tomorrow. Humans look upon facts as their truth but a fact is only a theory Man has been able to prove and remain a fact only as long as the theory remain proven. What goes up must come down, at one point in time was considered a fact, (truth). Since Man has developed fuels that generates the necessary thrust to propel missiles beyond the pull of gravity, what goes up must come down is no longer a fact. God's truths are not subject to change, whereas Man's truths are continually changing with out interruption.

.

BIBLE—THE BOOK

Has the teachings of the Bible made the world a better place? What would be the affect on the world if the teachings of the Bible and other religions disappeared? But for those religious industries that rely on religion for their existence and our lawyers whose profession is founded on the ideology presented in the Old Testament, (most of which was plagiarized from the codes of Hammurabi, Zoroaster and other earlier religions) would show that the Religions of the world, has influenced Human behavior toward good but little if at all.

Most Bible study groups focus on the Testament and Epistles in the Bible rather that it's origin. Seldom is the Bible itself, brought up as a subject for study. If we can accept this book as the words of God, then accepting what we find in the book is easy. Many of us are so engrossed in the study of the contents of the Bible, we give little thought to the book it self. Were we to study the Bible without any preconceived ideas of its content, we would have to question the reliability of its authors. They ask us to accept a conclusion our God given reason tells us is unreasonable. It is said this can be done through faith—for faith eliminates the need for reason. History has proven that faith in and of it self, has no value whatsoever. Many people had faith in Hitler.

The Evangelizing of Christianity had to overcome many obstacles as it traveled throughout foreign lands. Devoted missionaries, teaching what they believe to be the words of God, persuaded several people of the world, to embrace Christianity as their very own religion, They felt that the teaching of Jesus Christ's words would create a feeling of brotherhood so binding that we would feel obligated to be our brothers keeper. However, we must be ever mindful of the fact that what the Missionaries taught the Gentiles of the world was not the teachings of Jesus the Christ but the theology of Apostle Paul. Jesus taught belief in God, Peace, Love, Kindness and do unto others as you would have them do unto you, Love ye one another as I have love you, Thy Kingdom come, thy will be done, on earth as it is in heaven, for you will be judged by your good works. Paul came along a generation later, and said good works are as filthy rags. He distorted the simple message of Jesus the Christ from Belief, Love and kindness, to pray, praise and warship. In his epistles to his constituencies, he made the belief in Christianity complicated and difficult to understand. The magnificent castles and churches you find in Europe that took as many as tree hundred to build and the palatial churches you find here in the United States, is the direct result of the teachings of Apostle Paul who emphasize rituals and places of warship rather than the teachings of Jesus the Christ. The old order of the Amish community, thought it better to warship in their homes rather than build elaborate churches. Jesus said, "If two or more gather in my name, there I will be alas." (Matthew 18:-20

The horrors of the Medieval European inquisitions and the Salem Witch Hunts of early America could not reoccur. The teachings of Jesus Christ would help us evolve into civilized Human Beings. However nothing compares to the Holocaust that occurred during the twentieth century—committed by a nation that considered itself both Civilized and Christian. The atrocities, prior to the twentieth century, were committed in an attempt to establish Christianity as the world's religion. The atrocities, in the twentieth century, were an attempt to eliminate all those who practice the Jewish faith and to establish a new world order called the Third Reich.

EPICUREAN

The Quest for Pleasure

Western Civilization gives lip service to the Golden Rule and the ethical code of "In God We Trust," when in fact our culture embraces a capitalist system that demands its citizens compete for their subsistence. Our culture have made a deity of the dollar and justified the most ruthless labor practices imaginable—all in the name of corporate profit. We have developed a complete new language, a jargon that makes what is being done to the American worker palatable. Mergers, Down-sizing, corporate-restructuring, faze-outs are part of the new vernacular that justifies sending millions of American jobs over seas in search of a cheaper labor market. This is done for the soul purpose of enhancing the bottom line. Middle age men and women who have worked for a particular company twenty to thirty years or more, find themselves without a job and little prospect of finding another that pays a living wage. "Life Liberty and the Pursuit of Happiness," is the inalienable right of every American. As a private citizen in a capitalist, market-driven competitive economy, you have the right to whatever personal property your ability may amass. The deaf, dump, lame, blind, stupid, sick and just plain laze, can only expect whatever the competent members of our society allow to spill over after their cups are filled. It's called "Trickle-down." The thinking is, that a rising tide, lift all boats equally—which only applies if you have a boat. Where as, the Communist doctrine states, "From Every One According To Their Ability and to every one according To Their Needs." Although Communist claims to be Atheist, it seems to be more applicable to the Christian ethic, then, "the survival of the fittest," mind-set, found in the market-driven, competitive economy, of the Capitalist system. Capitalism and Christianity are as compatible as oil and water. Were Christ to return to the very culture that created Him, He would be labeled, a Bleeding-Heart, Liberal, and Communist.

Our ethic resembles most closely those of the Epicurean Principles that declares, God plays no part in human affairs or in the phenomena of Nature. Therefore we can live our lives of greed, envy and selfishness, free from superstitious fear of the unknown and the threat of divine retribution. Eat drink and be merry, for tomorrow we may be dead. What other explanation could there be for the embracing of Christian ethics in theory and the Epicurean philosophy, in fact. It makes one question the Sincerity of our religious and political leaders and what possible positive relevance they could have on our lives.

INTOLERANCE

Mankind must be ever mindful of the fact that nature owes no part of its existence to Human Beings. The universe, functioned quit well before the appearance of Man and if the dinosaurs are any indication, will continue to function long after we are gone. Mankind is not essential to the nature order of things. Our inflated egos do not allow us to accept the fact that we are only indispensable to each other. The Catholics fighting the Protestants in Ireland, the Hindus fighting the Muslims in India, the Serbs fighting the Bosnians in Sarajevo, the Taliban and Al-qaede declaring a Jihad on the entire world, is a direct result of each religion's insistence that their understanding of God and Creation is unequivocal and is the only one that must be adhered to.

Let us stop the religious gymnastics and direct these intellectual energies in ways that may produce positive results. These on going debates between the religions is a luxury we can no longer afford and must be looked upon as intellectual entertainment, to be indulged in only when one has nothing better to do. Our existence on this plaint is a reality, be it the result of some Divine Intelligence's will, or an evolutionary happenstance. We are all here with the same basic needed. The only known is that, we are born, we procreate, and we die. What is not known is what we should do in the interim. When a man falls in the water, his primary concern is swimming. How he got there, why he's there, who put him there, does not matter, he must swim or drown.

To try to restrict the behavioral patterns of an entire world and place them within the confines of a particular religion, is not very realistic. Mankind is not capable of the all encompassing love described in this religion. Our capacity to love is restricted by our ability to chose, which is prejudiced by our immediate environment, i.e., I love my Mother, Father, Sister, Brother, wife, children etc., more than I love yours. Mankind can only exist for me after them. This indiscriminate universal love is outside the realm of Human possibility. Love is a term used to justify preferential treatment towards a particular person or group—thus setting that person or group apart from the masses. Several cultures have no word for this concept. Until we answer yet to the proposition, "am I my brother keeper." Until we recognize the absurdity of these ideas, we will never be able to attempt a realistic approach to our problems. The greatest good we can do, is to realize the need we have for one another other—not love but need. There are people we are incapable of loving.

It is time we recognize the need we have for each other and not emphasize the differences that cause the confusion that separate us one from the other. What is needed is a universal concept of whatever it was that created us. The joy, sorrow, pleasure, pain, fear and wonder experienced by all Mankind, could be a catalyst to bind us together for the mutual good of all. We must not let fear of the unknown keep us from trying a new approach to the problems that confront modern civilization. The fears of falling and loud noises are the only fears we are born with,—all others are learned.

Let us began our new approach to the unknown by being less emphatic about our particular religious persuasion and recognize the fact that no one religion is more valid than another. Having done that, let us proceed by stressing what is within our ability to understand and what is self evident. We should show our appreciation for the gift of life by being honest, decent, kind, caring and allowing others to be the same. We must never let our egos become so comfortable with our particular belief that we try to impose them on others. Let us commit ourselves to being the best person we can be, try not to hurt anyone, and have the approval of our conscience in all we do. By doing this, when we die, where ever we go, I'm sure that is where we are supposed to be.

PHILOSOPHY

Nearly all the technological accomplishments of the seventeenth, eighteenth, and nineteenth centuries were surpassed during the latter part of the twentieth century. We have come to a point in time whereby we can virtually double our technical information every seven years. Unfortunately, the world's technicians, engineers and scientists, only strive to increase our creature comforts so as to improve the corporate bottom line, or assist the Military in killing people and braking things more economically. Now that the entire World has become (through the internet, and other technologies), one huge market-place, the other industrialized nations of the World are now motivated to indulge in this money making rat race. This foolishness in time will destroy us all.

Dwight D. Eisenhower our Thirty Fourth President, in his farewell speech said, "We must guard against the unwarranted influence the military/industrial complexes have throughout the world." Because of this misplace power, the potential for disaster is more imminent.

If our world is to survive, a hold must be placed on our technical research and development, in order to allow us time to develop a philosophy that will help us apply our technology in a less destructive way. Our present situation is similar to a handgranade being place in the play pen of a two year old—the explosion is inevitable. We must make an effort to devote more of our know-how, time, money and energy, to developing a philosophy that recognize the danger our runaway technology presents. If Mankind is to coexist with his fellow Man on this planet, he must resist the centuries of constant Religious bombardments that has been (and still is), the cause of most of the wars down through the years.

We need not discard any of the religions nor deter any one from practicing the theology of their chose. What is needed is an honest affords to make us more mindful of the fact that the same amount of importance place on religion must be place on developing a philosophy that emphasis how imperative it is that we learn to get along with one another, if we are to survive this Twenty First Century.

UNIVERSAL TRUTH

The only known is that we know not.
We know not from whence we came.
We know not the essence of—or the reason for our existence.
We know not the cause of our existence, (we only believe).

From these three known, let us develop a philosophy that
eliminate any need for the hypocrisy that allows Man to profess to
know the unknowable and justify this hypocrisy by saying, "this I
believe and the fact that I believe it makes it so."

PART 2

"Origin of King James Version of the Holy Bible."

The King James Version of the Holy Bible was not a book that just dropped out of the sky and was laying there in the sand, for the Jewish people to stumble over. No! The King James Version Of The holy Bible, is a collection of books, that took forty divinely inspired men, fifteen hundred years, to records the more than four thousand years of the history, culture, and laws of the Jewish People. It consisted of an Old and New Testament. The thirty nine books of the Old Testament tells us of the Creation and the Sins of Adam and Eve that caused man's fall from God's grace, the devastating flood during the time of Noah and God's promise to Abraham. It also prophesied the coming of a Messiah that by sacrificing his life would render man worthy of God's forgiveness.

The first five books of the Old Testament are Genesis, Exodus, Leviticus, Numbers and Deuteronomy. It is know as the Pentateuch. The Torah (history) and Talmud (law) can also found in the Old Testament. Many Theologians believe the book of Genesis was written by Moses although Genesis ends some three centuries before Moses was borne. The slaves in Egypt, practicing the Jewish faith, were referred to as Israelites. During the four hundred years of slavery, they became known by that name. It was a Hebrew called Moses, wise in the ways of Egypt and inspired by God, who was able to persuaded Pharaoh to release the Israelites from slavery. The phenomenal crossing of the Red sea during their exit from Egypt, convince them that they were truly God's chosen people.

The scriptures tell us that after crossing the Red Sea, the Children of Israel roam the dessert now know as Saudi Arabia for forty years.

During their odyssey through the Arabian dessert, God entrusted Moses with the Ten Commandments and the responsibility of sharing this information with the children of Israel. The Ten Commandments was place in the Ark that became the sacred covenant between God and man. Moses died at the age of One Hundred And Twenty. Before his death, he entrusted the leadership of the Children of Israel to Joshua who promise to continue the journey to the land God promised Abraham called Cannon. Joshua, lead the Children of Israel across the Jordon River to the west bank. He conquered all the tribes in that area along with the city of Jericho. Although Joshua was victorious in his conquest of these lands, it was King David who successfully untied Israel in the north with Judah, (later became known as Judea), in the south, that created the Nation of Israel.

When King Solomon, the Son of David began his rein over Israel, he was known through out the region as a very wise King. Other rulers paid homage to him by bring gift of gold, silver, ivory, mahogany and many other materials that he used to build a palace unparalleled in its magnificence. Although he was King of all Israel, Solomon decided to build this sacred temple in the city-state of Jerusalem.

The tabernacle King Solomon had built inside this palace was intended to be the final resting place for God's Ark of the Covenant. During the years of itinerant, the Children of Israel were able to protect the sanctity of the Ark until 586 BC when Nebuchadnezzar King of Babylon, destroyed Jerusalem and brought the Jews back to Babylon as slaves. He also ravaged the temple of Solomon and carried away all the sacred Relics found there, including the Ark of the Covenant, (That has not been found to this day). King Cyrus of Persia defeated the King of Babylon and issued a decree allowing the Jews to return to Jerusalem to rebuild the Temple destroyed by Nebuchadnezzar King of Babylonia. The second temple, built on the same site as the first, was Finish in 516BC.The impact of the completion of the second temple stimulated the Jewish People and made them more stead fast in their Faith.

The Old Testament ends with Malachi and between Malachi and Matthew, (the first book of the New Testament), the K/J/V/ of the Holy Bible is silent. This four hundred year void was instrumental in the development of the New Testament.

The Philosopher Socrates, student Plato, had a pupil name Aristotle who tutored Alexander the Great, the conqueror of the known world at that time. Although Alexander the Great was born in Macedonia, he was considered Greek and was instrumental in exposing those conquered regions to the Hellenistic culture that practice polytheism, (the belief in more than one God).

Before the decline and fall of the Roman Empire, there were twelve emperors of Rome, yet the K/J/V/ of the Holy Bible only concerned it self with the first five. They were Caesar Augustus, (not to be confused with his uncle Julius, who after Alexander's death, captured all the conquests of Alexander plus the British Isles) Then their was Tiberius, Caligula, Claudius and Nero. A crazier group of people can not be found any where in recorded history. Their desire to be considered God and not mere mortals may have had something to do with there psychosis. Caesar Augustus appointed Pontius Pilate governor of the city-state of Jerusalem.

Before any of the Sanhedrin council decisions could be implemented, it must first be approved by the Roman Governor Pontius Pilate. Therefore, it became his responsible to preside over the trial of Jesus the Christ. After hearing the charges brought against Jesus, he found none of them was contrary to Rome law hence he left it in the hands of the Sanhedrin council.

The Sanhedrin council was not unlike our present day halls of congress, in that it had two political parties with different views. The Sadducees much like our Republican party were conservative and dedicated to maintaining the status quo. The Pharisees were more open to change and resemble our Democratic party in their liberal views. However, the Sadducees view prevailed and Jesus was convicted of blasphemy and sentence to death by crucifixion. Not until a spire was thrust in his side was he declared dead and place in a tomb form which it is alleged, he emerged three days later.

After the death of Jesus the Christ, his disciples continued to spread his word through out the eastern shores of the Mediterranean

Sea. The Canaan land God promise Abraham, that was once the land of the Philistines, Phoenician, Palestinians and now is Israel, were the most influenced by his teachings. His word also spread to southern Europe, where the people were known as Gentiles. A Gentile is anyone not practicing the Jewish Faith. However, Paul only exposed this new religion to the Gentiles of Southern Europe and those areas bordering the eastern shores of the Mediterranean Sea.

By this time, Nero had become Empire of Rome and the Monotheism taught by Jesus the Christ had spread through out the Roman Empire. This could not be tolerated, because Nero thought he was the one true God. His response to this new religion was to command his solders to round up all the followers of Christ and have then brought back to Rome and thrown in the arena to be eaten by Lions as entertainment. Even these drastic measures did not deter the followers of Jesus from spreading his word.

There was a man name Saul, (referred to as Paul in the K/J/V/ of the Holy Bible), who live in Tarsus, a city in South East Turkey, that was exceedingly well versed in the Torah and Talmud of the Jewish religion. He was also a Roman Citizen due to his home being in Tarsus that was a part of the Roman Empire at that time. He had been very successful at persecuting the followers of Christ when one day on the road to Damascus, he was struck down and a vision of Jesus the Christ appeared to him and said "Paul why persecute thou me?" Paul responded by saying, "what would thou have me do?" "Go and it will be reveal to you." In spite of the efforts of Paul and Nero's Solders, the message of Jesus the Christ continue to spread through out the Roman Empire because Jesus message was simple and easy to understand, therefore, the masses follow him in droves.

His message was, LOVE THE LORD THY GOD WITH ALL THY HEART, SOUL, MIND AND BODY, LOVE YE ONE ANOTHER AS I HAVE LOVED YOU—AND DO UNTO OTHERS AS YOU WOULD HAVE THEM DO UNTO YOU. His entire message is summed up in those few words that can be found in the book of Mathew 22: 37 through 40. This is the message Jesus handed down to Peter by saying "upon this rock I build my church." Some feel that the success Paul had in persuading Peter that Gentiles need not be circumcised in order to be followers of Christ, lead him to believe that he was the one chosen to take this new religion to the Gentiles. Paul traveled over the areas known as Asia Miner (presently called the Middle East) also Southern Europe four times spreading his Pauline theology while neglecting the Near East and Northern Africa. The continue spread of this new religion so irritated Nero, that he had Peter and Paul brought to Roma and executed, Paul was decapitated and Peter crucified upside down. However, Know where in recorded history is their evidence of this happening. The teachings of Jesus the Christ continued to spread and attract more followers.

Not until Constantine, in 313 accepted the Edict of Milan, (which removed all penalties for being a Christian), was Christianity accepted as the official Religion of the Roman Empire and Christians were no longer persecuted. Contrary to popular opinion neither Peter nor Paul were the first Pope, Constantine was the first Roman Emperor to be recognized as Pope and as Pope, he felt a New Testament was needed. Therefore, he surrounded himself with Scribes, Bishops, Ecclesiarch and High Priests, authorizing then to canonize any books of the Apocrypha they felt were compatible with the teachings of Jesus the Christ, They selected Matthew, Mark,

Luke, and John as the books that most accurately describe the life and times of Jesus the Christ. The book of Matthew was written by Matthew, one of the twelve Apostles, who walked and talking with Jesus during his life on earth. John also was one of the twelve Apostles of Jesus. He wrote the book of John plus three epistles alone with the Book of Revelations.

Mark was not one of the Apostles and there is no evidence that he ever saw Christ. Some say he was in the garden of Gethsemane when Peter cut off the ear of the high priest servant and Jesus restored it but this could not be confirmed. Over time, Mark and Peter became quite close, on occasion Peter would refer to Mark as his son. The book of Mark, was written by Mark and much of the information found there was the result of his close relationship with Peter who was one of the twelve Apostles who walked and talked with Jesus the Christ.

Luke also not one of the twelve Apostles, was a successful physician and historian. Luke wrote the book of Luke and as the youngest of the authors of the Gospel, acquired much of his information from the renowned historian, Flavius Josephus. Luke also wrote the Book of Acts summarizing the accomplishment of Paul. All though Paul is often referred to as "Apostle Paul," he was not one of the twelve Apostles of Jesus the Christ. Jesus was crucified three years before Paul was born. The remainder of the New Testament consisted of fourteen epistles by Paul, one by James, two by Peter, Three by John, the book of Jude and the book of Revelation written by John who also wrote the book of John that is part of the Gospel. These books and epistles constitute the New Testament. The books written by the other Apostles, that walked and talked with Jesus, Simon,

Thomas, Thaddaeus, Philip and Bartholomew, may be found in those books of the Apocrypha that were not chosen to be part of the New Testament.

Five hundred and seventy two years after the death of Jesus the Christ, Muhammad was born in the city of Mecca in the country now known as Saudi Arabia. Tradition has it that at the age of forty on the mount of Hiram the Arch Angel Gabriel called Muhammad and told him that Allah had appointed him the messenger to preach the truth about the oneness of God. By the year Seven Hundred A/D, Muhammad had founded one of the largest and most recent religions to teach the monotheism of God. The Islamic Bible is called the Koran. Abraham, the original teacher of the oneness of God, had been dead more than two thousand years and Jesus The Christ, along with his Apostles had been dead well over four hundred years before Muhammad was born. The Islam religion flourish in those areas Paul neglected to bring the teachings of Jesus the Christ. This New Religion that was accepted in North Africa, the Near East and the southern part of Europe. continued to spread until it reach the Himalayan Mountain range which beyond them, has well established religions such as Hinduism, Buddhism, Confucianism, etc., that was much older than both Christianity and Islam.

Martin Luther (1483-1546) founder of the Protestant Movement was a German priest, monk, theologian and university professor.

He agreed with the Pauline Theology that preached, "Only though faith in Jesus and not good works could man be redeemed from his sins." In 1517, he began his protest by publishing his 95 theses that rail against the teaching that salvation could be bought. Martin Luther's anti-Semitic views were instrumental in promoting the conduct of the German Nazi Party that advocated the burning of synagogues, destroying Jewish prayer books, forbidding rabbis from preaching, seizing Jews' property, money and smashing their homes. From 1930 to 1945, Hitler's German, ruled by the Nazi Party, took Martin Luther's suggestion and followed them to the letter.

The protest of Martin Luther was the foundation by which other denomination, formulated there own interpretation of the K/J/V of the Holy Bible. It was the protest of Martin Luther that influenced King James of England to have the Bible translation from German to English in the same way the Old Testament was translated from Hebrew to Latin (Greek). This was known as the Septuagint. As Shakespeare was a contemporary of King James and the most fluent in the English language, many feel that he was chosen to do the exegesis of the hermeneutics of the interpretation.(in plain English it means) the examination of the translation but I found no evidence of this.

The first printing of the English New Testament was in 1525, most of which was taken from the Tyndale Bible. From the Second Century through the twentieth, there was several Version of the Old and New Testament written. The K/J/V of the Holy Bible as we know it today appeared in 1611 AD.

The fact that God created the world and everything therein (including man) is a given. He also gave man the ability to reason. Is it reasonable to believe that God revealed his existence to a chosen few and gave them the responsibility of spreading this information to the rest of the world? Would it not be more reasonable to believe that if God wanted man to know of him, would he not have given this information to all mankind, for them to believe as they choosen?

PART 3

"Americans of African Descent Exposure to Christianity"

The purpose of this commentary is to identify what is true and—correct the half-truths, assumption and out and out lies as they relate to Americans of African Descent. For years, we have associated our ancestry with ethnic groups that in no way represent the American of African Descent. Some of our most prominent leaders have led us to believe that we are in some way related to those Biblical characters found in the Old and New Testament. That is total nonsense. Nothing could be further from the truth. If you believe in the Bible and use it as a reference, it becomes obvious that this religion originated with Abraham, Isaac, Jacob and Esau. These people were Arabs, some times referred to as Hebrew, Semites, Israelites or Jews. The name Jew does not apply because anyone practicing the Jewish faith is considered a Jew. Africa was mention in the Old Testament twice. Once when Moses led the Children of Israel out of Egypt, and again when Sheba, the Queen of Ethiopia known as the Queen From the south, and to her own people as Makeda the Beautiful, travel to Jerusalem to pay homage to King Solomon. These two occasions were the only time Africa was mention in the KJV of the Holy Bible.

Contrary to popular opinion, Africa is not a Monolith. The different histories, cultures, languages, dialects, art and rituals practiced throughout the vase regions of Africa are too numerous to count. Northern Africa, known as the Maghrib consists of Egypt, Libya, Morocco, Tunisia, Algeria, and Mauritania, is distinctly different from Sub-Sahara Africa. The difference is due to the influence the Greek and Roman culture had on the Maghrib, when they brought it across the Mediterranean Sea into Northern Africa. The countries of the Middle East, Near East and North Africa, make up a major part of the Arab World.

The historians and scribes of Europe officially recognized Piankli as the third ruler of the twenty-fifth dynasty of Egypt in 753 BC. He is recognized as the Pharaoh who united Nubia, Meroe, Hush, and Egypt into the great Nubian Kingdom that stretched from Ethiopia north to the Mediterranean Sea. From the first Pharaoh of Egypt Menes (Mens) 3100 B.C. to Emperor Haile Selassie of Ethiopia, who died in 1974, this land was govern by African men of color. However, none of the major religions of the western world, Christianity, Judaism or Islam ever penetrated south of Ethiopia into Sub-Sahara Africa. The history, cultures, languages, Dialects, art, and rituals of these regions, were left completely undisturbed for thousands of years until the coming of slavery.

With the discovery of Central, North and South America, along with the islands of the Caribbean, the Monarchies of Europe became aware of products they never know existed such as cotton, indigo, coco, Tobacco and Sugar. As these produces are labor intensives and the Monarchies of Europe were demanding more and more of them, it became apparent that a labor force capable of withstanding the cruel conditions surrounding the growing and harvesting of these products was needed. The indigenous people of these areas of the Western Hemisphere, were incapable of enduring the kind of horribly intensive slave labor required for this task. The exact reason for the demise of the Incas, Aztec and Mayan Nations, is not known but I'm sure the Caucasians of Europe attempt to enslave them, along with the many diseases brought from Europe that the immune systems of the indigenous inhabitants of these regions could not cope with was a determining factor.

It is documented that the African slave trade began in 1441 at the hands of the Portuguese. Not long thereafter, they were joined by the Spanish, French, Dutch and English as slave traders. When they realize the native of Sup-Sahara Africa could endure the more than six thousand mile, five month trip from the coast of West Africa to the island ports of the Caribbean Sea, later to the southern ports of the united States, they were no longer considered human beings; they were now looked upon only as black gold. They were placed below the decks of cargo ships and stacked like cords of wood side by side one against the other in order to be assured the ship was filled to capacity. No where in Antiquity can be found such inhuman treatment as that bestowed on the Africans as they were transported from Africa to the Western Hemisphere. That they survived this horrid treatment and still maintained their concept of self worth and did not allowed them selves to be persuaded that they were little more than cords of wood, speak volumes as to the mental and physical stamina of the inhabitance of Sub Sahara Africa. They are the true ancestors of the Americans of African decent. A/A/D/.

The United States was a late comer to the slave trade. This was due to the many problems it had establishing itself as a sovereign Nation. In April, 1803, the leader of the slave revolt in Haiti, Toussaint L'Ouverture, through deception was capture and deported to France where he died of pneumonia while imprisoned at Fort de Joux. After his death, Toussaintl'Ouverture's two chief Lieutenants, Jean Jacques Dessalines and Henri Christophe took over the Haitian army of slaves and defeated the French at the battle of Vertieres. As Napoleon could no longer maintain a garrison in Haiti, and was unable to protect his possessions in the United States, he agreed to the Louisiana Purchase which allowed much of the land west of the Mississippi River to be considered part of the united States. In 1815, with the help of the pirate Jean Baptists Lafitte, General Andrew Jackson was able to defend the city of New Orleans against the British, thus making the boarders of the United States more secure, whereby they could now concentrate on producing products that could be sold in markets throughout the World. The demand for cotton, sugar, tobacco and other products grown mainly in the southern part of the Unites States, made the need for Slaves more apparent. Although the United States was late in entering the Slave trade, she extracted more slave from West and Central Africa than all the other countries combined. By 1860, the more than 3.8 million Africans enslaved in the southern states of America accounted for one third of the population. These slaves had been separated from their Religion, History, Heritage, Culture, Traditions and Language for more than Four hundred. Because their culture never felt the need for an alphabet, none was developed. Their Religion, History, Culture and Heritage was handed down from one generation to the next by Griottes. A Griot is one who memorizes the history and heritage of the village and then hands it down to the next member of the village designated as the Griot. Alex Haley's award winning book Roots, was the result of his going to Gambia West Africa, sitting patiently day after day listening to a Griot until he heard the name Kunta Kinte, the name he needed to connect this American slave to his roots in Africa.

By introducing slaves to Christianity and only exposing them to pages of the Bible that made them more docile and easier to manage, the slave masters felt Christianity had been very helpful in maintaining the practice of slavery. They appease their conscience by saying, "they were merely doing their Christian duty by introducing savages to Christ" With the passing of time, the history, culture and language of the Slaves brought to America were forgotten and replaced by the Religion and Language but not the culture of the United States. Although they were torn from their roots, they never forget their cultures concept of family. The African Slave conformed to the Christian religion simple because there was no other religion available to them at that time.

Down through the years, the negative portrayal of the American of African Decent by the Citizens of the United States has caused many A/A/D/ to reach out to other cultures for a positive image of themselves. Cassius Clay (a.k.a.) Mohammed Ali, Kareem Abdul Jabber, Elijah Mohammed, and many others, are example of A/A/D/ attempting to divorce himself from the deplorable image concocted by American Citizens and replacing it with a portrayal that is more positive. In their quest, they embraced a culture, history, and heritage that do not apply to him. Yes, it is permissible to select the religious persuasion you are most comfortable with but it does not affect who you are. A/A/D/ looking for names that indicate a positive image need look no further than Sub Sahara Africa, where names like Dedan Kimathi and Joe Moe Kenyatta (leaders of the Mau Mau revolt in Kenya), or Wunyabari O Maloba (Authority on East African History), or Dikembe Mutumbo and Hakeem Olajuwon (NBA Basket Ball Players) were prevalence. These names are like rolling claps of thunder during a raging spring rain, reeking with masculinity. When Malcolm Little, one of the leaders of the Islamic movement in the United States, realized he had no idea what his African name may have been, he was honest enough to called himself MALCOLM X.

A/A/D/ feel that because of the Bible's reference to Egypt and Ethiopia, which is in Africa, they concluded that in some way, this is part of their heritage. Nothing could be further from the truth. The regions referred to in the Bible, (North Africa, the Middle East and some parts of Southern Europe), only confirms the fact that the ethnic groups involved were not Sub Sahara Africans. They were Caucasian, Arabs, Hebrews and Semites. Some may feel that Jews should be included in this group but Jews are not an ethnic race—a Jew is anyone practicing the Jewish faith.

Contrary to popular belief, Africa is not monolithic it is not all the same. It is a Continent not a Country! There are More countries found within the borders of Africa, than in any other continent on earth. However, when most people think of Africa, they think of it as a Country with one culture and that culture applies to all of Africa. Therefore, it is permissible to embrace any of the African cultures and referred to it as their own. The American of African descent A/A/D/ need not look to other cultures for a positive image of themselves. Throughout Antiquity, no other ethnic group have proven themselves to be more civilized than the Black men and women of America. They are the only people while sojourning in a country that they were not indigenous to, was able to bring about a change to the racist polices practice by the United States, without the use of bloodshed. Dr Martin Luther King said, "We will correct this injustice and if blood must be shed let it be ours."

Both the Old and New Testament approved of the existence of slavery, the right that one man has to own another. When mention in the Bible, it only gave reference to its existence but never condemned it as an example of man's inhumanity to man. Paul's epistle to the Ephesians Chapter 6, verse 5 said, "Be obedient to them that are your master with fear and trembling." In spite of this, we adopted Christianity as our faith for we know of no other at that point in time.

The first Americans of African Descent, A/A/D, was brought to the United States in 1619, a year before the Mayflower. At that time they were considered indenture servants. Those that followed came in chains as slaves. It is time the United States citizens realize that this is as much their country as any other ethnic group. They were here long before the industrial revolution of the 19th and 20th centuries brought the immigrants from Central and Eastern Europe to the United States. In order to emphasize the difference between the descendants of slaves and the rest of the population, Americans of African Descendant, has been referred to as Colored, Negro, Blacks and African American. The most accurate description of the descendants of slaves born in the United States is, American of African Descent. They were born here in the United State, Not in Africa, Here! They manage to survive the horrible conditions on the slave ships that brought them here, slavery, the antebellum area, Jim Crow, the Ku Klux Klan, segregation and racial prejudice. They fought in all the wars and were the economic base for this country's success during its early year. During the Civil War, there were 185,000 Black Soldiers in the Union Army, 37,638 lost their lives while participating in 39 major engagements, Sixteen Black Soldiers received the Congressional metal of honor. When Dorie Miller received the Navy Cross for downing four Japanese planes during the attack on Pearl harbor, many Americans thought there was little to no history of Americans of Africa Decent in the U.S. Navy. However, at that time, it was a little known fact that by the year 1860, there were 29,511 Black Sailors in the United on States Navy. By the end of the Civil War, the Union Navy had awarded four Black Sailors the Congressional Medal of Honor for their gallantry in action. Only three years after the repeal of slavery, On July 13, 1868, Oscar J. Dunn a former slave became Lieutenant Governor of Louisiana. The Americans of African Decent also created JAZZ, the only art form recognized through out the World, as originating in the United States. There is no other art form attributed exclusively to the United States of America.

When Rosa Parks stood up in that bus and said, "I'm not going to take this any more," and rallied a nonviolent army around her, lead by Dr, Martin Luther King Jr., that caused the strongest nation in the world to change its racial policies (against its will), shell go down in history as one of mankind's greatest accomplishment. The irony is that they were able to do this by following a religion that was new to them and that religion embraced slavery. They as a people went from slavery to the White house in less than a hundred and fifty years. So when you are looking for a positive image of your selves, you need look no further than the history of the United States of America.

The accomplishments of your ancestors down through the years, in spite of the unbelievable harsh conditions they experienced, have made it possible for you to stand tall, look any man in the eye and say I am proud to be an AMERICAN OF AFRICAN DECENT. (AAD).